Swastikas and Crosses

ROSHAN B. KARKI

DEDICATION

To everyone who knows me as Roshan B. Karki !

CONTENTS

ACKNOWLEDGMENTS

This book and all the characters are based on my imagination. No part of this publication, including its text and plates, may be reproduced in any form without prior permission in writing from the publishers.

POEMS ABOUT LIFE, JOURNEY AND PARTYING

A Bottle of Wine

Let the day turn to dusk and moon shine.
We are on table and there is bottle of wine.
Our wishes will come alive tonight and
drinking wine is my only dream this night.

Today it's Christmas
Cheers to the bottle of wine!

The next week will be New Year's Eve
Cheers to the bottle of wine!

The following month will be Valentine's Day
Cheers to the bottle of wine!

The day after six months will be our anniversary
Cheers to the bottle of wine!

Let the moon shine.

A Day Lived Fully

A day will come in everyone's life
A day full of life and vigor
A day that is lived fully
And that day is enough
To be remembered for life time.

It may be a marriage or a honeymoon.
It may be walk in rain on monsoon.
The day lights in your heart like a bonfire.
Everyone has a certain day;
a day that is lived fully.

So share your pictures. What is there to worry?
Since that day I am half of century already.
I am old but bold.
That day lights up in my heart like a bonfire.

A Game of Cards

Let the cards flip
and let the brain cells be activated.
We are in round table waging wars.
Cause we are playing a game of cards.

The power of king is pure
but the queen in locked in an ivory tower.
It's been five hours since we are on table.
Cause we are playing a game of cards.

Your money now belongs to me.
Its midnight and tides are unhappy in the sea.
Let there be fun and joy.
Cause we are playing a game of cards.
And we want to pass the night doing so.

A Lost Paradise

Remember
when we were kids
we used to make paper boats
and sink in streams.
We used to fly kites
till then night approached.
We used to play with wooden swords
and make our own empire.
I used to hold your hand and say,
"You be queen. I will be king."
Now the things are different
You are gone
and waves have erased your footprints.
The flower in garden
which you used to put in hair
is decayed and defrosted.
We are in different worlds now.
And years we were together,
and dreams we dreamed for forever
is a lost paradise.

Agony

Ask me my friends what is agony?
I know what it is.
I feel it's bombarding in my mind
when I see sadness in your eyes.
And each minute the teardrops
Falls like rain on the seas
Like snowflake on glaciers
And each drop of snowflake
Ramble in my mind
When I see sadness in your eyes.

At a Discotheque

The music howled
And the footsteps marched
Across the crowd
And I found you all alone.

I bought you a drink
The night passed within a blink
And we stopped at a motel
Tired with red eyes.

The following morning you were gone
Without letting me know
The night passed strangely
The night passed like a miracle
Hey stranger, I thank you dear

High school Parties

We used to buy cheap liquor
with a fake id
And we used to hurry to basement
To play beer pong.

Then life was nothing much
Except parties and studies
The cheap beer now tastes bitter
But back then it was delicious
And it added life to us.

I remember those days
I look at pictures in Friday nights and ask,
" Where are you?
And what happened to our eyes."

Mysterious Highways

I do not know where this highway will lead.
I am all alone in my car.
I have driven miles so far.

The river by is flowing swiftly.
I do not know where the river goes.
The river goes to the sea.
But where do the mysterious highway go?

A city must be waiting for me.
The lights in skyscrapers
must be wild in nights.
May be I should just trust my instinct
and go along the mysterious highways
all alone in the nights.

Old man in a Bar

I met an old man in a bar
drinking wine with water.
His faces had scars
telling the stories untold.

He had seen peace rallies and wars.
He had kissed his lover.
His children and grandchildren live somewhere
but he is all alone in a bar.

The liquor makes his mind more concentrated.
His life now belong to Gods.
He is hopeless yet romantic.
as he drinks wine alone in a bar.

POEMS ABOUT MYTHICAL SUBJECTS, EVENT AND PEOPLE

At a Church

I passed a church
Where Jesus laid
The people said,
"Those who believe in him
Will be free from suffering."

But I felt cruelty
but I felt beauty
And strength of a faith
So me on a Christmas day
Went to Church
To wish Jesus happy birthday

That night
Jesus came in my eyes
While I was sleeping
And said,
"I am a legend.
Every day is my birthday.
Celebrate life
Everyday like your birthday.
I will be there for you."

Dubuque Port

Let the ships sail
Like they always have been
Doing in my mind
They float like dreams.

The crews are partying
Ring the bells
The midnight is here
And I am watching the Dubuque Port.

And as the night passes
The tides will be high
Let the ships sail
I am in Dubuque Port.

Hallelujah

(Inspired by Leonard Cohen's Song Hallelujah)

The king is tired of entertainment.
He somehow envy's them.
He wants to dance and sing
And he is singing hallelujah.

The battles have just started yet
The does not care for it
He is looking at the battle field
And he is singing hallelujah.

He has a palace
and a beautiful queen.
The battle is over now.
He is singing halleluiah.

The moon is on the sky.
He is drunk watching the tides.
He wants to give his kingdom away.
And just sing hallelujah.

Legends

They will ride on horses of death.
They will sleep with pretty women in bed.
Faith will be together as a shed.
There will be ghost riders and angels.
Let the bells jingle.
Let the history repeat and prove.
The legends will never wither.

There deeds will be blood written in pages.
They will walk with kings. They will walk with sages
Cause the earth will be home of legends.
Travelling as ghost riders. Travelling on dragons.
They will drink wine with angels.
There soul will float like feathers.
The legends will never wither.

My Horse Changed into a Unicorn

There was a bottle of wine in my table.
My horse was tied up in a stable.
Did the moon casted a spell?
There was a ring of a bell

Was I drunk I thought for a minute?
A unicorn was in the shed.
My horse had changed into a unicorn.
It was white and had a horn.

My horse rode with me in many wars and bars.
Now I have a unicorn gifted by gods.
I will travel it with it to heave and along the universe.
I will drink wine in bars of mars.

My horse changed into a unicorn

Never Ending Path

Life is a never ending path
through years, heaven and eternity.
And we must walk our walks
walking along the gold paved streets
and place where dogs bark.

Is there another world?
It's a hope. It's a dream
but no one knows and have seen
what lies on other side of the door.
Cause life is a never ending path,
you live your life fully
there will be another life once more.

Our Civilization Lay

The west has Jesus
The east has Buddha
Between their teachings
Our civilization lay.

The west has skyscrapers
The east has temples
Between the statues
Our civilization lay.

The west has faith and love
The east has faith and love
Between the enigma
Our civilization lay.

Quest for Immortality

I understand the enigma of immortality
The body is just a vehicle
And soul is the driver.
You change your destination
from a world to other.
Immortality is just processing of matter.
This is first way to be immortal.
Writing good sonnets, stories and songs
will make you remember for ages
Like Dante, Homer and Shakespeare.
This is second way to be immortal.

Statue of a Poet

Yet he laments
What the world is becoming
His eyes has tears
That can be felt
But cannot be seen.

He lays
On a side of bus stop
Thousands people pass by him
And he is almighty
But no one can see
He is in tears
And watching the streets.

Hey people
make him cheerful
For he has already
Paid his vows
Let the statue smile.

Tales of Snowmen

The snowmen
Came alive in Christmas
The army of snowmen
Walked in town.

They said, "No one cares about us.
Winter is cold and
People do not put us jackets.
People mock us and make fun of us."

People in home were
Drinking wine
They make snowmen
Out alone in moon shine.

So they decided to complain Jesus in heaven.
The Jesus from heaven said, "
"I am so sorry.
They treat you so cruel
on my birthday.
Go live in poles.
You have a continent of your own."

That's how Antarctica was formed.

The Night Rider

The night rider
goes from kingdom to kingdom
receiving and giving news.
He has covered himself with scarf.
His dress are black like the night.
He does not care if he is hungry or thirsty.
He is loyal to the Emperor.
He rides in storm and the moon.
He fears there will be a war soon.
The emperor pays him good fortune
and that's enough for his family and him.
When he appears there will be ring of bell
He believes in Jesus in nails.
The dragons fly with him in skies.
But each night the ghosts and demons come alive.

And with darkness you have to pay the price.

POEMS ABOUT LOVE

23

As the Couples Walk

As the couples walk
I feel I want to be them
They talk their talks
And I somehow I envy them.

You are perfect for me
Let there be beauty
And golden dreams
As we walk together.

The moon in here
And lovers are in the sky
They are happy and high
As we walk in town.

As the Wind Blows

Don't let the wind blow our love away.
It's fall. The wind blows.

Don't you let your eyeliners fade away
It's fall. The wind blows.

Don't let your heart go away.
it's fall. The wind blows.

Let the wind blow and hold my hand.
We will go together anywhere the wind blows.

Forever Mine

You were meant to be mine.
Our shadows will be together in sun shine.
We kiss as if we are bound to the sea.
And we will live in a yellow submarine.

The nymphs sing and the bed is with corals.
But they are cheaper than our love.
Our submarine flows from sea to sea.
And in sea bed we will be never tired.

Porcelain Ceramics

I am a porcelain ceramic
More than flesh and blood
Each hour, each second
Makes me hungry for love.

We drink tea together
on a cup of porcelain ceramics.
You be me. I will be you.
We are hungry for love.

We are pieces of porcelain ceramics.

When you are with me

I feel I win the world
when we walk together in pavements
holding our hands. I feel invincible
when you are with me.

The stars guide us. The moon shines for us.
The people gaze us and feel happy.
I feel heaven when you are with me.
Our bond is invincible.

Let us make our own kingdom of love.
The crows, crowd and the mob cheer for us.
We will be together in each other's arm.
I feel invincible when you are with me.

POEMS ABOUT WARS

One Last Time

Raise the sails up high.
Let the dragons fly in the sky.
We will ride for war
this time and for last time.

After we reach the shore
we will burn our ships.
Let there be no choice else victory.
We will ride to wars for the last time.

Let the moons gaze our bravery.
We will charge with our infantry.
Let the history remember this day.
We will ride for war this one last time.

Search for Forces

I entered a tunnel
Searching for mystic forces
To meet with Goddess
Living there.

The Goddess asked me,
"What do you desire?"
I said, "I have fame and fortune.
But I want to be invincible."

So I made an army
Blessed by the goddess
That never loses
To create a better world.

The battlefield is ugly
The swords are stained with blood
There is only desire here
to move with my army with invincibility.

The Royal Infantry

Tit for tat. Dust for dust
My Royal Infantry represents the United States.
We ride on finest horse.
It is an army made for single purpose,
to make goodness and justice prevail on earth.

We can charge from one to ten.
We fight in days
and dream of our victory in tents.
My royal infantry is bravest force on earth.

So let the horn blow
and we ride for victory once more.
We have won tens of wars
and we will keep on winning
unless I command my royal infantry.

POEMS ABOUT POLITICS

History is not Far away

I look myself in a mirror.
My face has wrinkles
and my soul has experiences.
History is not far away.

I lead the world for living
I work hard from dawn to dusk
There are thousands reasons
You will remember me.
History is not far away.

And my children will share my legacy.
I believe in humanity and love.
Will I be a legend?
The history is not far away.

Leaders of Next Generation

Is there a generation gap I wonder?
Our generation belongs to music
from Katy Perry to Taylor Swift.
Some call us indigo children.
We are leaders of next generation.

God have given us power of vision.
These visions will someday rule the world.
We will solve wars, poverty and famine.
We are leaders of next generation.

Strange Times

The world needs more heroes
It's dwelling in strange times
But just like every day
The sun appears and the moon shines.

Let humanity be a religion.
The world can be God's Kingdom.
We are dwelling in strange times.
The world can be yours and mine.

So I will talk talks
with beggars and kings.
We will make humanity
a religion
because we are dwelling in strange times.

Swastikas and Crosses

I entered a garden.
The trees were made of bones.
There were swastikas and crosses
hanging on the wall.

To east- swastikas are crosses.
to west- Swastikas are curse.
But the cross is same everywhere.

The visitors bowed and prayed
to swastikas and crosses.
I am from east. They mean same to me.
And Hitler was a devil
who misused Swastikas from the east (from
Hinduism)
and conducted genocides.

The cross granted their desire
whatever they might be.
The world is full of
Swastikas and crosses.

POEMS ABOUT ME

A Home in the Sky

I want to build a home in the sky.
Near the place where moon lies.
The home will be my satellite.
And I will watch the stars as they pass by.

I will look up every night.
The blue ball will look lovelier ever.
The moon will be here. The stars will be near.
As I drink wine looking at earth from the sky.

As the Time Floats

Slowly the needles
Dance in the walls
They were floating since
I was born
And will be dancing
When I will get old

The needles
Do not know
Day and night
But I know

And the needles dance since then.

I Belong to the Myths

The humanity came from chimpanzees
that changed odors and colors.
But I belong to the stars in the sky.
As I fly with dragons in my mind.
I belong to the myths.

The pages of history are tempting
as I am sailing a ship.
And the tides are hungry jumping.
Take me to treasures and wonders ship
because I belong less to you and more to the myths.

In my Mind

Each day
what dwells in my mind
comes alive at night
when the moon is on sight.
The dreams fly like kites
as if it's my soul
travelling to other world
when I keep dreaming
dreams of angels and fairies
that will come alive each night
and leave me the following morning .

Know your Worth

39

I know my worth
I am worthy of resorts,
Beaches and fine cars.

I know my worth
I am worthy of love
Duty and hope.

I know my worth
If I don't succeed today
I will do it tomorrow or someday.

I know my worth
I belong to humanity
History and mankind.

Man and the Mask

There can be thousand masks
but my face will be the same.
There might be thousands days
and my affection will never change.

I will put mask on your face.
I will put one in mine.
Let the stars glitter
and we look each other when the moon shine.

We will walk on crowded streets
where everyone is wearing masks.
We will be hungry for love
from dawn to dusk.

We both wear masks.
The god designed.

Man and the Myth

Let people say
I fly with dragons
aiming heaven
far from blue sky.
And I command my troops
while I come in news
as a hero
solving wars and famine
and give justice to the world.
Fortune favor me.
I pay power
with honesty and loyalty.
At night when the
full moon is on the sky
I haunt vampires
and spend the night
with my princess.

I am a man with a myth.

Poetry changed my life

42

If my poems mean anything to you,
Those who read it are lot
And live it are a few.
I am not very rich
But I have everything a human being
Will desire.
I have enough paper and ink
My mind ferments poems like
Wine in a jar.
I paint beautiful verses on paper.
The verses are as beautiful as nature.
Writing poetry changed my life.

Read Poetry

The blood like ink
Floats slowly like river

The ink like words
Tear like the Sea

The waves in the sea
come to me

As I read poetry

September 27th

Let the sun rays dazzle the sea
and spark like diamonds
with your beauty. Because it's Sep 27th.
It's our anniversary.

I have kissed you deepest in the nights.
And will be with you and it's a light
I am a president
and you are the first lady.
Together we will go to history.
It's Sep 27th. It's our anniversary.

Let the soldiers move forward
and acknowledge your command.
It's Sep 27th. Today let the world celebrate
our love and beauty. Today is our anniversary.

Snakes in my Dreams

Sober! I lie in bed
and my soul travels
across time and space
I have dreamed
this dream before
It's howling
It's haunting
waiting for something
As I see snakes in my dreams

Thank you United States

Thank you United States
You have given me everything
And I will never leave you till the end.

I had nothing
I now have something
Thank you my mother.
You have showered me with affection.
I feel so fortunate to be your son.
Thank you United States
I will never leave you till the end.

The Dream Dreamed Last Night

I saw myself in a dream.
I was wearing a diamond ring.
I dreamed a dream
As a human being
and to fulfill it was my only dream.
People dance and sing
about the dream I dreamed.
I could go to pages of books forever
and the dream is enough for life long.

The Dusk

The dusk is perfect time
to meditate and write poems.
The city floats like feather in the sky.
And I glance it from my room and
the reflection of couples kissing in pair
are in the skies.
My soul travels to different world.
And my hand grabs a pen and paper
and reflect the sky on papers like a mirror.
The pets are out.
The bar is crowded.
But I sit still in my room
looking at the reflection on the sky.
The moon passes by.
The angels fly.
And God in heaven must be cheerful
looking down below in the sky
and I mediate and write poems.

The Golden Dream

The golden dream
Sails on horizon
All I ever wanted
Is to be together with you

What are years?
Let them pass swiftly with vigor
And life be like stars in nights
Our kiss will float
like feathers in the sky.

Verse on Paper

Can you separate blood from ink?
I cannot. They mean same to me.
Blood flows in my veins.
The ink float on papers.

The pen in very clever.
It's emptying my mind out.
But as the blood floats
the paper becomes kind.

The paper is so kind.
each page leaves a tale behind.
You are only thing in my mind
and you come out as beautiful verses.

The verses are as beautiful as you.

ABOUT THE AUTHOR

Roshan B. Karki (Roshan Bikram Kark) is a poet, writer, musician, entrepreneur and politician. He was born in Kathmandu, Nepal. He has attended Loras College, USA as an honors student to pursue undergraduate in Creative writing. "Swastikas and Crosses " is twenty second book by the author. He publishes his book independently via create space. Although he is an Asian his creative sources include western writers and western philosophy. His books have appeared worldwide on major online websites. His major genres are poetry, science fiction, political science and fantasy. In the coming days with the help from readers he aims to publish his books physically and go on world tours reading poetry. Please give his books a read and welcome the new genre of writing!